This anthology offers an alphabetical collection of 26 word portraits uncovering the failings, exploits, and dreams of everyday hopeful, murderous, glamorous, desperate, real women-next-door.

Timeframe: May 1964 - May 2018

Setting: from Cape Town, South Africa over Taipei, Taiwan & passing through Basel, Switzerland.

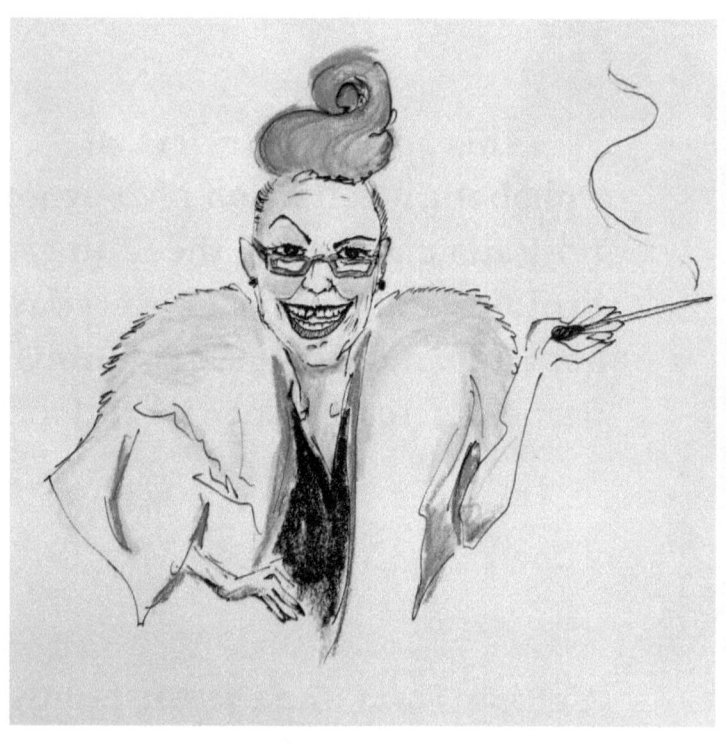

The authoress, as seen by a tactful colleague

Ansi Verwey - von Fleckenstein

BOUNCE BACK BABES

26 word portraits of real women

©2019 Ansi Verwey - von Fleckenstein
Author: Ansi Verwey - von Fleckenstein

Cover painted by PEDRITO
Editor: Anonymous BOSH

Back page: original art by ANSI. She recommends this image as protection against a lack of contentment, coffee or decorum. Mental application of the sketch guarantees immunity to charlatans.

ISBN: 978-3-7497-7781-5 (Paperback)
ISBN: 978-3-7497-7782-2 (Hardcover)
ISBN: 978-3-7497-7783-9 (e-Book)
Publisher & Print: tredition GmbH, Halenreie 40-44, 22359 Hamburg

Das Werk, einschließlich seiner Teile, ist urheberrechtlich geschützt. Jede Verwertung ist ohne Zustimmung des Verlages und des Autors unzulässig. Dies gilt insbesondere für die elektronische oder sonstige Vervielfältigung, Übersetzung, Verbreitung und öffentliche Zugänglichmachung.

Motivating guardian angels, without whom this book would not have been possible:

Anonymous Bosh, Sofia Pavone, Michael Rath, Matthias & Peter Wegele, Emiro von Berejesa †2019, Katja & Hannah Beer, Bianca Gierok, Ralf H. Dorweiler, Elena Filipova, Michael Leibundgut, Phoebe Lin, Eva Buffoni, Gerda Pretorius, Helga Karen, Hinako Yoshikawa, Iryna Krasnovska, Lussys von Scajuka †2018, Ivan Konsulov, Raquel Rey Ramos, Shalini Treffer, Yuval Zorn, Armando Braswell.

INDEX

1. Aurora und Arnauld in the KUMQUAT Store..11

2. Brigitte Brandt: No Black Eye in the Brocki.........14

3. Cordelia and the charming chandelier................18

4. Donna researches job alternatives......................20

5. Eva's ghosts at the watering hole.......................22

6. Frene: in search of yogurt..................................23

7. **GIULIA'S SUMMER COLLECTION: a pocket** True Crime Story...24

8. Excerpt from the chronicles of Hilda..................26

9. Isolde and the quest for the ideal man................28

10. Red Juliane's Unified Theory of Colour 31

11. Kerstin's Cat: A Song of Lamentation with a Funeral attachment.................................34

12. Literary Leonie's Silverfish................................37

13. Martine researches men 42

14. Grouchy Nora...45

15. Olivia at the opera....................................50

16. Petra pulverises the Monday blues.............52

17. Visiting quirky Queenie..........................54

18. Regina's racehorse....................................56

19. Sleepless on Sophia's sofa.........................57

20. Tina at the Tinguely Fountain....................59

21. Uschi at the dentist.................................62

22. Veronika; life in bite-sized portions............63

23. Wilhelmine wanders the woods..................69

24. XANTHIPPE 71

25. Yolinda's Yodelling Horn..........................75

26. Zippy Zoë...78

PROLOGUE

This collection of portraits of REAL WOMEN is my homage and thanksgiving to all the PROUD BROADS* who have inspired me through the last five decades and helped me keep my focus firmly on the silver lining - NO MATTER how many dark clouds threaten to suck the joy out of life. From Day One my grandmother determined: every cloud has its silver lining.

These short life sketches are Portraits of Events covering ground from Cape Town (South Africa) to Basel (Switzerland) between May1964 and May 2018 that **PROUD BROADS***, experienced, wished, dreamed, grew out of the habit of and brought to the table.

*PROUD BROAD (German: VOLLWEIB) is a positive expression, in this context: a female being who daily discovers her femininity, expresses and defines it anew - with her iPhone in her bra and emancipation in the air.

HARD WON INSOUCIANCE
a self-portrait

Recently a cheery lady in her seventies served me up a double-edged compliment when she asked, with all the earnestness of a wartime presidential interviewer: "How do you manage to waltz through life in such carefree fashion?"

Twelve years ago such a question would have had me on the floor quietly giggling and drooling until the nice men in white coats gently took me to a padded pink rubber room.

As we now live in 2019, any potential jaw-dropping on my part was arrested well short of the floor by my spontaneously rising interrogatory eyebrow.

Had I just been attacked by a compliment? Or was this another sign from the Universe not to take on too much at once?

After more than five decades of life spent collecting experiences, both desired and despised, inner reflection has developed an answer that saves me time and nerves, "How? Honestly - with ritual self-forgiveness the occasional small luxury, and regular amusement."

1. Aurora and Arnauld in the KUMQUAT Store[1*]

As she slipped into the amethyst-purple evening gown Aurora knew buying it would be more exciting than anything on offer in the KUMQUAT store over on Baseler Freie street. Not only did she have a weakness for the latest gadget from high-tech Mega-giant KUMQUAT, she also passionately loved draping herself in every imaginable jewel tone she could lay hands on.

The on-staff geniuses at KUMQUAT would make regular bets on how many times a month "Jewel Girl" would come in to make a purchase or get some advice about her K-Pad or K-Book. Aurora wasn't especially tech-savvy, and had the attention span of a frolicking golden retriever. After one of her visits a staff member abruptly decided to change careers and enter a monastery.

Seven weeks ago Aurora noticed her local KUMQUAT store's Consultation Department had hired a *very* decorative young frenchman. The brilliant Arnauld had that charming french gift of making any of the languages he spoke sound like a poor relation of his mother tongue. English, German, or even Russian: no matter, Arnauld's perfect grammar would be elegantly served in a crystal goblet of murky french vowels.

After Aurora finally snagged an appointment with Arnauld (who was much in demand), she spent sleepless nights trying to decide what to wear for the encounter.

[1*] Definition on page 13

The night before she dreamed in green, so she decided on a conservative emerald ensemble - accessorising her K-Book with a matching green case.

At 1:30 pm on the dot Aurora and Arnauld met at the KUMQUAT store to delve into the intricacies of her K-Pad Pro's picture editing program. Aurora was hypnotised by how the charming Frenchman took on the german language. Even under the clinical store lighting, the driest tech jargon seemed to her a symphony in the colours of every jewel tone she'd ever loved. Suddenly she noticed the wedding ring on Arnauld's hand. Totally distracted, she interrupted his flow of professional terminology by blurting out, "Is your wife french too?" Arnauld eyes lit up, "No, my husband is Italian."

That put an abrupt end to the post-graduate course in CGI. Arnauld just had to show Aurora photos of his magnificent Italian husband. Her chin dropped. The Italian dreamboat was wearing a velvet smoking jacket in the *exact* same shade of amethyst as her new evening dress! Using her huge photo library on the K-Pad Pro, she pulled it up to show Arnauld.

THERE IS NO SUCH THING AS COINCIDENCE!

Arnauld knew right away that the dress and the jacket, or rather Husband Alessandro and Jewel Girl Aurora had to get to know each other ASAP. "Could you come wear your amethyst dress to be the Conférencieuse at my husband's birthday party this Saturday?"

Aurora made a quick excuse and ran to her friend Google to ask just what a Conférencieuse does. "Conférencieuse, the female form of Conférencier: an amusing master-of-ceremonies in Variety, cabaret, revues, concerts radio and TV. As well as announcing the numbers, he/she entertains with jokes, funny poems, and songs."

T-H-E birthday party became legend. Since that evening Aurora, Arnauld and Alessandro are inseparable friends, loved and hated in the press as "The Three Amethysts".

Aurora, who now only works luxury conférencieuse gigs, had the amethyst dress framed. It hangs in her boudoir, a constant reminder that guardian angels also watch over wardrobe choice.

1 **KUMQUAT** store is a wholly fictional name. Until the author gets permission to use the name of a certain massive concern that doesn't sell fruit, that's her story and she's sticking to it.*

2. Brigitte Brandt:
No Black Eye in the Brocki[2*]

Brigitte shivered sadly in her chic, tailored B-cups. After twenty-five minutes of beating around the bush, her friend Ulla had finally dropped the bad news on her: Brocki, her combination stylist, interior decorator and happy hunting ground for the wonderfully odd presents she notoriously loved giving friends - was closing for good in seven days, another casualty in the battle against Amazon and Ebay.

This news threw Brigitte into deepest mourning. (Publishers Godawful & Gross's etiquette guide to the Brandt family's complicated bereavement protocols and customs has gone into a fifth edition.)
Brigitte took up her battered, dog-eared copy to make sure she didn't overlook anything. Tales of family members who failed to complete the rituals properly always ended dreadfully, and were told to scare the children on Halloween.

It is forbidden to write the rules down, that could call up evil spirits! The family legends were to be passed on STRICTLY ORALLY. Back in 1683 a grouchy old Brandt ancestor, Brechreuss IV, issued the BRANDT EDICT to ensure, under penalty of death, that the tradition conti-

---

[2*]Brocki: a second-hand or thrift store in Switzerland

nue. It is a measure of his influence that this edict will remain in force through 2020 on two continents.

Shock froze Brigitte's blood and drank the very tears from her eyes. Ulla, well-versed in dealing with the stages of grief, applied a few warm chapters from Nietzsche's THUS SPAKE ZARATHUSTRA[3*] to prevent further paralysis.

After two solid hours of Nietzsche, the first tears began to creep across Brigitte's coal black eyeliner, opening a small gate for the deluge of bitterness, disappointment, and suicidal thoughts that followed. Ulla did not have to dig around long in her well-organised purse for the ABSOLUTELY appropriate tissues (black-edged with a pattern of calla lilies) to blot up the fast-flowing tears. As a mother-of-three she was armed and ready for any emergency tissue situation: white for the innocent, Despicable Me minions decor for the uninspired, hot pink for cocktail accidents, and rainbow ones to keep hope alive.

Three and a half calla lily packs later Brigitte felt up to going for a last look at the future mausoleum, that is to say her favourite Brocki. Always a bit thrifty, Ulla persuaded Brigitte to wait instead until the last day of Brocki's going out of business sale. Before that the friends had to come up with some sort of substitute for the soon-to-be-no-more Brocki, otherwise they could be in mourning until next Christmas.

[3*] modern translation:
THUS SPOKE ZARATHUSTRA

Clever Ulla, aided by two bottles of champagne, convinced Brigitte to clean out her basement instead of looking for a new Brocki! Downstairs they went, through four generations worth of dead spiders' webs. Brigitte had kept going to Brocki to get more stuff without any thought of clearing out the old, so it took the girls FIVE WHOLE DAYS to get any kind of organisation in there.

And there it was: after it all got sorted out, the place looked just like Brocki in the Good Old Days!
The results were quickly photographed from all angles and posted for general admiration on Twitter, Instagram, *et al.*.

On Brocki's last day the two friends met up at the door wearing their Mourning Dance Slippers. Silently they joined the mass of nameless faces.

Practical Ulla held the big brown leather Lamentation Drum ready. It vibrated with their every step, automatically guiding their hands in the pulsating rhythms of grief.

The beat travelled along the floor under the crowd, lifting a foot here, testing a shoe there, found voice to translate itself, and finally infect the very air with the dance of self-healing that is our birthright.

3. Cordelia and the Charming Chandelier

After a hard day's work Cordelia walked obliviously down the street after a hard day's work. She was just about to give herself up to a dull gray existence when the chandelier threw a spanner into her well-oiled existence.

Its huge magnificence hung (firmly, in accordance with city safety codes) against a cloud-curtained sky so depressing that it had had all Europe's Suicide Hotlines working overtime for a solid month. Was the chandelier part of the last dregs of the cities' opulent Christmas decor…or maybe some sort of advertisement for one of the many restaurants the area?

Feeling a bit hungry, Cordelia stopped.

At that moment the sun broke through the clouds, its brazen rays cheekily shredding the ugly cotton blanket and tickling the chandelier's prisms until adventurous pearls of rainbow beads popped out of Cordelia's hair, rejoiced, and began nuzzling their way down her spine under her practical thick winter coat.

This unexpected magnificent back-massage motivated Cordelia to abruptly throw off her tired coat, her dull wool cap, dump her organic-politically-correct shopping on the ground, and dig her heels into a joyful Macarena. Dancing wildly, she realised she needed a new bathing suit …<u>THIS</u> <u>VERY</u> <u>INSTANT</u>!!

Snatching up her pitiful clump of winter clothes and groceries, still skipping lightly from the rainbow beads (now nestling contentedly between her toes), she threw herself headlong into shopping's pleasures.

She left the smiling chandelier behind her. The next fortunate victim of this out-sized street jewellery was a gentle, middle-aged lady who suddenly developed an aversion to her sensible Birkenstocks and chose to go buy her very first pair of high heels. Her Macarena tonight was sure to be an unforgettable performance!

On the way to work the next day Cordelia again passed "her" chandelier. Though this time no rainbow beads showered down, she stopped anyway to salute it with a quaint little boogie before bouncing off to work.

Under her staid winter clothing she wore an itsy-bitsy, teeny-weeny, rosy-pinky string bikini.

4. Donna Researches job alternatives

Recently Donna was abruptly sacked from her dream job in Basel, so she went straight to the red light district to inquire about vacancies. As one of the Freshly Unemployed she bubbled over with a torrent of innovative ideas about working in a completely new field. For her own inspiration and motivation she composed a list of her education, experience, and special talents so that she could speak about herself in job interviews professionally without inhibitions. Topping her list of capabilities: *"REALISING & ORGANISING THE DESIRED"*. Her 33 years as a children's book illustrator held no more interest for her.

Although before the day she had her first encounter with being fired Donna had had no experience in a red light district - long weekends in Amsterdam don't count - she thought that with her talent for organisation she could enjoy a life as an outstanding Madam. She imagined how it would be. First get an apprenticeship, then after 14 months as an intern she could begin her new dream job.

She went happily to the "Tolerance Zone" just a hop, skip, and a jump from the Rhine - what a great place for a new life! She was dreaming of her internship when Fate gave her a nudge. For the first time she noticed that Basel actually had official bureaucratic pavement markings and street signs designating the pleasure district. "How practical!", she thought - before her artist's eye objected. If you're going to mark out a a Tolerance Zone, why not use graphics directly appropriate to the history of the World's Oldest Profession? She began to think on a larger scale.

On her way to City Hall to inquire about the possibility of redesigning the Tolerance Zones's street signs, it hit her: the signs in the red light district weren't the only ones desperately in need of a « NEXT TOP MODEL »-style make-over. She was quite realistic about her creative ideas and knew that her project, the "TARTING UP STREET SIGNS INITIATIVE - T.U.S.S.I.", would never fly with the city Fathers and needed careful thought before the concept was unveiled to the public. She would need like-minded allies working with her, refining ideas to get this project off the ground.
She hopped an a bus to the Euro Airport and caught a discount flight to Berlin.

Stretched out on her childhood buddy Angela's Flokati carpet she tinkered with a greater global project that would make Donna the Coco Chanel of street sign graphics. In just a week a portfolio of proposed markers for every major metropolis was ready to be shipped.

Seven years hard work later Donna's street signs were "the little black dress" in every major city's wardrobe - an absolute *must*. She was recently commissioned to do the signs for Gaudi's Sagrada Familia cathedral in Barcelona.

So as NEVER to forget the humble beginnings of her new life, Donna always carries a picture of the Basler Tolerance Zone's sign with her in her signature giant handbag.

5. Eva's ghosts at the watering hole

How could I be dead
  when you were still alive,
    hating the reeking corpse
      clutched in the futility of spurned anger?

Why did you laugh
  when last I saw your scorched back
    receding into the naive stone
      all lovers might curse?

While you resisted the current,
the roots forgot their tree and also perished.
A virgin pool, ruptured by the perfect pebble,
strove for purity and was obliterated.

Your tree, drooping independent parasites,
  stared at the sky accusingly,
    throwing threatening arms at perfection.

A plastic bag, skimming the rotting leaves
  cleansed my senses of reality.

The distraught father went home to find an empty nest -
  and built another.

6. Frene: In Search of Yogurt

Frene always made a point of bagging the same prey on her grocery hunts: fruit, veggies, meat, bread and yogurt.

She confesses that she doesn't choose her store with an eye to frugality, popularity, or inventory. As she has no car, sheer geography dictates her shopping choice.

She most often uses the supermarket about 70 yards from her workplace - although it's well known that glorious swarms of six legged hardcore lambada-dancing vermin gather there to party away their last days.

She sticks with HER store (for convenience and to protect the innocent, we'll just call it EUROPEST) because EUROPEST is directly on the streetcar line that takes her to her apartment (affectionately called PESTOPIA by friends). Her choice of supermarket may also have something to do with the omnipresence of that adorable, rugged, stud-muffinly security guard with the deliciously threatening MATRIX-style.

Frene knows she would die happy if she could just work up the courage to shoplift a little something from EUROPEST.

7. GIULIA'S SUMMER COLLECTION,
a pocket True Crime Story
Subtitle: no good deed goes unpunished

Anyone exercising their dog near the Lange Erlen Zoo Park in Basel would think that Giulia and her two golden cocker spaniels are a permanent fixture. Giulia, a devoted dog owner, didn't just give her doggies Giorgio and Givenchy three short, perfunctory walkies daily, no! Every trip to the park was a lush opportunity for the hyperactive pair to bounce around, be admired, get some training practice and grooming too. It was well known that Giulia invested about a third of her income into her dogs and was on a first name basis with all the pet store owners in town.

But for three weeks neither Giulia nor Giorgio and Givenchy had been seen at the dog park.

The result of an investigation follows:

On a sunny Wednesday morning Giulia strolled to the station to catch her usual commuter train to work. As she stood in line at her favourite coffee kiosk for a cup of caffeine-rich motivation she couldn't help but notice the very proper businessman in front of her was experiencing catastrophic deodorant failure.

From childhood Giulia's life had been complicated by her unusually sharp sense of smell, so she always carried an Emergency Deodorant Failure Aid kit ready in her giant battered purse. She didn't want to intrude, but when she noticed the aromatically-disadvantaged victim on the platform waiting to get on her same car, she couldn't contain herself.

Had she known that just 40 minutes ago Gottfried's [for that was his name] wife had been shrieking at him about an ongoing tax audit and his rotten personal hygiene poor Giulia would still be alive today. It's a pity that the security camera footage can't be put up on Youtube: it's got to be Oscar-worthy.

Giulia readied her little pink Emergency Deodorant Failure Aid (EDFA) to relieve the sufferer as smoothly as possible. Packet in hand she moved decisively toward the lightly quivering Gottfried just as a through train was announced. As she expertly and thoroughly explained the EDFA contents and their use, Gottfried eyed her stonily from behind a clenched, crooked smile.

Suddenly he snatched her up in a tight, full-body hug and jumped in the path of the onrushing train. In the instant before she and the odiferous Gottfried were spattered, mashed and scattered, a choking Giulia was still smiling with confidence that she had saved another B.O. victim.

Postnote: *Giorgio and Givenchy live happily in Hannover with their Doggiegodparents Matty and Petronella. They can regularly be seen frolicking around the Eilenreide park.*

8. Excerpt from the Chronicles of Hilda
- Death in the afternoon

She flopped into her favourite chair on the heavenly green terrace next to a giant marble ashtray, sullenly staring at the first snowflakes as they drifted down to earth and death.

A lost swallow fluttered over the roofs, a definite harbinger of the next rail strike.
Obviously a soulmate who had pulled up stakes and moved house without noticing the warning signs of change. Two involuntary tears of sympathy spilled over Hilda's clenched cheeks and landed in the overflowing ashtray. She lacked the energy even to decide whether or not to light the next cigarette.

She daydreamed about her festive entry into Shoe Heaven. She saw herself floating barefoot through the Heavenly Gates wearing a simple, shimmering sheath gown. A strange feeling of security roused her from her half-sleep. By the ashtray, a joyously dying swallow lay in the snow. An orange tabby tomcat was giving its soul the last rites.

Oblivious to his high office the tom turned to attend to his union-mandated morning toilette.

While the small soul of the happy swallow set off to knock on Heaven's gate, the orange tabby undertook a half hour's thorough washing of his right front paw. In the course of a regulation day's straying it's amazing what all can make itself at home between toes!

As with painstaking pleasure the tabby cleaned the last bloody traces of the ashtray swallow (and relatives) from between his second and third claw, a wandering sunbeam fell across the neck of the fresh little corpse.

Thus could the astonished swallow's soul blunder into paradise astride the ghostly path of an errant ray of sunshine.

Moral of the story:
When beside an ashtray in the snow,
expect no help from any stray tabby cats.

9. Isolde Seeks Her Dream Man

In the almost two decades since her divorce from Urs (everyone should mistakenly contract a short, wild, hormone-driven mistake of a marriage at least once, RIGHT?) Isolde has been searching for the 80-60-40 dream man recommended by those experienced in marriage as a sport.

For the uninitiated: This man should
- be at least 80 years old,
- have at least 60 billion ready cash (for shopping),
- register a 40° Celsius fever…and
live conveniently close to an understaffed Intensive Care Unit (ICU).

Naturally Mr. 80-60-40 should have no legitimate heirs, and ideally bestow a title on his future widow. "Countess" would suffice, "Princess" is a bit much, as royal inheritances could involve tiresome political complications and duties.

Yesterday Isolde had a rendezvous with a well-qualified candidate. In bed last night she leafed through her large bedside collection of bridal magazines and, sure enough, found a designer to her taste. She immediately booked an appointment online.

For the last twenty years, right up to the moment she fell asleep on this auspicious occasion, Isolde had single-mindedly dedicated her every free minute to one hobby: **The Search for The Dream Man.**

Her bored unconscious mind ambushed her dreams and handed her an overdue reckoning.

Isolde dreamed she was buying toilet paper. No sooner had she painstakingly chosen the right color, thickness, perfume and print when she was handed a tiny, long-haired dachshund puppy. In his bright brown innocent eyes the urgent need for walkies was written so clearly that Isolde dropped the carefully chosen TP rolls and took off to find some grass for sweet doggie relief.

In her wild plunge for the door she was joined by her clinically-depressed son in full goth gear. Three black lipstick-smeared duty kisses were delivered when she suddenly found herself in a dusty, shabby store where they rediscovered the mother-son bond while rooting around in search of toilet paper. The other customers in the post-apocalyptic retail outlet were all 13-year old girls doused with an overdose of sickly sweet perfume, wearing strict victorian clothing and garish Tretchikov-style eye makeup.

After an extensive rummage through the unlikely assortment of wares - from car parts to sailboat tackle to exotic groceries, Isolde suddenly found herself standing with a pair of spiky gladiator sandals instead of the intended toilet paper in her hand. Engrossed in the joy of shoes, she didn't notice the threatening change in the atmosphere as sobbing Tretchikov girls pushed past her.

The colourful customers stampeded to the back of the room in a panic that increased as they tried to hide themselves from a tango-stomping shadow holding a reliable pistol with which it was tattooing the mass of panicking shoppers. Isolde threw herself to the ground too - the gladiator stilettos safely clutched to her bosom. As she smelled the sharp metallic odour of fresh blood, she was not sure if her son were the gunman or the victim.

Her own resounding scream of utter desperation ripped her from the nightmare sleep! She flung the bridal magazines in the recycling bin and cancelled her appointment with the couturier.

From now on she will be devoting every free minute to family and friends.

10. Red Juliane's Unified Theory of Color

Between Juliane and the color red it was anything but a case of love at first sight. Hadn't her mother's all red kitchen repeatedly sent her into fits of nightmares as a child? It was only after her ten-year-long "Black is King" phase that she developed a preference for all things scarlet.

The black phase had begun during her career as chartered accountant. Shortly after finishing her studies she found a good job with a company famous for avoiding economic risks. Her close work relationship with Josef from the cubicle next to hers led (after a proper twelve month engagement) to an unexciting, practical marriage. Since Josef preferred wearing black and both were lazy housekeepers, not at all interested in separating laundry, they settled for functional black clothing - preferably unisex.

Her red phase started fairly quietly with a red lipstick, a gift from her husband who could no longer stand the sight of Juliane's pale face in the ocean of black clothes. As a last resort Josef chose to present her with a cherry red luxury-lipstick instead of divorce papers.

Applying the red lipstick worked a small wonder: for the first time since being traumatised by her mother's red kitchen, Juliane could look at herself in the mirror without shame or rage. It was as if the cherry red lip color crawled directly into her limp veins and flowed through them, destroying absolutely every "anti-red" intention in her jaded body and replacing them with a jaunty spring fever. When later that day she *just had* to buy lipstick-matching pantyhose - WITHOUT ASKING JOSEF's OPINION, it was all over. That very evening she donated half of the couple's shared BLACK ONLY wardrobe to charity and forced a patient Josef to look at pictures with her for hours: red cars, dresses, houses, and shoes.

So began Juliane's Age of Red. The couple's hard-won status quo would have held if she hadn't been such a passionate gardener. In her black days she was content with a manicured lawn, some rocks, and carefully selected cacti. She used to meticulously slice the head off any cactus blossom that dared show itself.

Josef, who was secretly deliciously amused at his Lady Wife and deeply desired a cactus-free garden, was also influenced by the red objects appearing in and around the house. For their eleventh wedding anniversary, he planned a supremely gaudy surprise. After months of meticulous research, he found the ultimate present: a weekend in England's brightest, most colourful rose garden.

Through his connections with the British Rose Mafia, he had made contact with an extremely eccentric lady in southwest England whose life's ambition was to make a rose garden containing every single hue known to man. In June she allowed a few people whose first name began with "J" to book weekend stays. The low price for this package vacation was explained when arriving guests were informed of the mandatory minimum of four hours daily labor in the huge rose garden.

The garden work was overseen by four spoiled corgis whose complicated care was also part of the deal. Let's just say that this sojourn was the foundation of Juliane's Unified Theory of Color: **ALL COLORS GO TOGETHER!**

This romantic weekend (where, by the way, the first of two sets of twins were conceived) unleashed Juliane's Color Revolution on her immediate vicinity.
Starting with her now favorite color she began emphasising it with accessories in tones that contrasted with the joyful palette of cherry red. She discovered that screaming purple went better with red when a pop of green fluttered over it and the look was "grounded" with topaz gold shoes.

Friends and co-workers, noticing Juliane's change of color and attitude, began striking up conversations with her about the WHEN and WHY, as well as practical applications of her Unified Theory of Color Flexibility. After a while these casual chats on what can only be called an uncontroversial subject began to bridge failures of communication between friends, spouses, and co-workers; even defusing situations at political gatherings that might have led to lynchings.

After the birth of a second set of twins Juliane ran for mayor and was voted in unanimously.
At the moment Juliane is working on an effective Chromatic Solution to the Middle East Conflict.

One thing you can count on with this politician: her panties remain practical and cherry red.

11. Kerstin's Cat:
A Song of Lamentation with a
Funeral attachment

On January third at 8:45 AM Kerstin looked deep into the tormented blue eyes of Katja, her 18 year old cat. She yearned for her grandfather so strongly, that he ripped apart the fragile veil between life and death and stayed next to the death bed, preparing Kerstin for the end of Katja's life.

In constant pain during the last years of his life, not even Grandpa Simon could smile the traces of agony out of his eyes. It took courage for a twelve year old Kirsten to meet his tormented gaze. Her dearest wish had been that her own smile might tickle the pain out of his poor old crooked body.

Slowly and steadily rubbing Katja's paws in farewell, she could feel the sedative caress the pain out of the tight little body as the drug mercifully changed pain to gentle sleep. Kerstin and softly purring Katja looked into each other's souls as they shared that moment of freedom. A drowsy, almost playful touch of a paw to Kerstin's ring finger, then Katja faded away into sweet rest.

As the first tears threatened to drop Kerstin to the floor, Klaus, the vet who was to give the second injection[4*] that would send Katja to the eternal catnip fields came in. Since he was seven years old he'd wanted to be a tax consultant. But coming from a famous family of veterinarians, and lacking the strength to contradict them, he'd had no real choice of profession. After he graduated (naturally, summa cum laude, as was expected of him) he set to work at the family clinic with uninspired competence.

He had no empathy with animals or their owners: to him they were numbers, part of the his clinical statistics. Making lists & tables of treatments, euthanasias, time & motion efficiency and such was how he kept a bit of his accounting dreams alive.

As Klaus efficiently set about giving the lethal injection, he realised that his week's euthanasia numbers would be above the average and was secretly proud of his neat calculations. Kerstin's weeping over her pet being put to sleep, well *that* was entirely average.

He was looking forward to adjusting his spreadsheets when the distraught Kerstin stopped him to invite him to her beloved cat's memorial service. As he had not yet

---

[4*] *These days most vets put down an animal using two injections: the first to make the animal drowsy, the second to set them free. This allows the animal's owner a last chance to watch their pet fall peacefully asleep before then seeing their friend off on his final way.*

compiled statistics on cat burial rites, and wanted the quickest possible escape from yet another sobbing woman, he accepted.

Being well-bred, he came to the Rhine riverbank gathering with homemade funeral cookies, his grandmother's recipe. He'd added a pinch of catnip to the dough - partly as a joke, but also to see if it might give humans a bit of that feline high.

Not really outgoing by nature, Klaus was somewhat intimidated as pink champagne was pressed on him and he was introduced to the colourful funeral guests. His hope for anonymity was shattered by Kerstin's terribly esoteric demand that each guest step to the water, sprinkle some cat fur, and speak their deepest personal wish so that Katja could fulfil it on her way into the Beyond.

Not wanting to be conspicuous, Klaus went over and told the Rhine as well as the supposed feline soul in transit that he really wanted to be a tax consultant.

Eight years later Tax Consultant Klaus and cat-less Kerstin are happily wed. What started with cat funeral statistics became a rollicking marriage, producing the twins Katrin and Conrad.

The kids just won't stop begging for a kitty.

12. Literary Leonie's Silverfish

One might say it's quite indecent how much Leonie reads. Almost every other young woman her age moves over to iBooks, iPad or some other darn i-Incarnation of the i-Infernal i-Family. And now there's a whole legion of girls who've sacrificed reading altogether in the name of **Meatfix**[5] addiction. Thus Leonie finds an ever-growing offer of books pleading to be « adopted » from sadly neglected bookstores.

Leonie's relationship with books started in her childhood when she suffered from every possible allergy. On her seventh birthday her parents gave her a golden cocker spaniel. One overly friendly lick from the hyperactive puppy sent her to the emergency room. It took three days of treatment before she could breathe normally again. Her first night home, a stray cat wandered into her bedroom through her wide-open window. One touch of its inquiring paw sent her back to the ER with running eyes, breathing difficulty, and an aggressive case of hives.

---

[5]* **Meatfix:** Is a generic name for video portals. These providers encourage their customers to replace the habit of reading with zombie-like staring at a fascinating variety of TV series and film - in other words to **fix** your brain so it's just **meat** between your ears, hence "Meatfix". Leonie cancelled her subscription when she learned that Meatfix users gain an average of 6,3 kilograms per month of mindless gawking.

The doctor on call, Dr. Grimmgold, had Leonie tested for every imaginable allergy and was perversely delighted with her results: no one had ever seen or documented such a rare collection of extreme allergies! He knew that Leonie's condition could make him world famous in all the medical journals.

After a serious conversation, the parents accepted that home schooling and a strict vegan diet were the only possible remedy for Leonie's explosion of allergies. Dr Grimmgold gave Leonie her first encyclopaedia, an older edition of "ALLERGY TREATMENT - THE BASICS" that he had read to tatters as a young med student. He only wanted to cheer her up, and was blissfully unaware of the side effects his present would cause.

In her sterile bedroom Leonie thought she had to read the book as quickly as possible. If an authority figure with magical healing powers like Dr Grimmgold handed her a book like that, then maybe it could take away her allergies! She still had a touching belief in miracles.

But no matter how hard poor little Leonie struggled to read herself healthy, her allergies bloomed and mutated into new varieties of the classic pollen and dust-mite allergies, resisting all the weird and wonderful treatments Leonie was subjected to. Leonie, sporting her standard uniform of scrub cap, gloves and full respiratory mask, studied "her" encyclopaedia with hope and gritted teeth.
In order to understand the enormous book, she started hunting for copies of ALL the other books cited or even briefly mentioned in « her » Encyclopaedia of Allergies.

The ghostly pale, wheezing little girl was soon well known to all the antiquarian booksellers in town.

Leopold was her favourite bookseller, though. Because he worried at little Leonie's lack of normal childhood experiences, he threw in a colourful book suitable for kids with every dull medical text she selected.

The turning point of Leonie's lonely life came when Leopold gave her an antique magnifying glass that had belonged to his father - to help her study the Asterix comics he kept springing on her. He hoped that she would find something to giggle about in the brilliant little details so cleverly hidden in the corners of the drawings. It was obvious that her sterile homeschooling did not extend to a class on basic smiling and its cousin, a sense of humour.

In her cloistered library of a bedroom, Leonie picked up the magnifying glass to study the Asterix comic closely, as Leopold suggested. She screwed up her deathly pale brow in concentration…and there, between pages 1 and 2, she discovered the first living creature that didn't trigger her allergies: a playful little silverfish.

Her sheltered tutoring had not even mentioned the *concept* of "vermin", so Leonie could observe the tiny insect without any sensations of disgust. Under magnification it seemed to be enjoying the funny pictures as its shimmering little body frolicked around on the page.
Leonie promptly christened her newfound roommate "Idéfix" because it seemed to favour Obelix's fluffy little dog in her Asterix comic. A careful search found a who-

le little non-gallic village of silverfish getting to know Asterix, Obelix and Miraculix first hand.

She hurried back to Leopold's store to find out more about her first pet. Leopold looked at the shining eyes of the pale little girl who demanded to learn EVERYTHING about silverfish and remembered that by chance he did have just the right book on hand. In the rusty safe were he kept all the books he thought he'd never sell, he found "THE SILVER SWARM" for Leonie.

This collection casting silverfish as protagonists of heroic legends was written in 1854 by a prisoner serving a life-sentence in the dungeon.

Motivated by loneliness and a fascinating collection of mental disorders the convict studied in detail the only living creatures he had contact with in his humid, warm dungeon and raised them up as heroes in his tales. The prologue to the book had the key data on the "artists": silverfish have 6 legs, and 5 antennae. They reach a maximum length of 0.9 inches (a modern 2,28 cm) and can live as long as 8 years.

When Leonie read that her flock of friends would also eat allergy causing mildew and dust-mites, a life-long friendship was guaranteed.

Armed with new knowledge, Leonie made sure that her room, and later her own house would have optimal conditions for silverfish. Since her little playmates needed a temperature between 20 and 30 degrees Celsius and high humidity to reproduce well, Leonie insisted on cultivating a small indoors semi-tropical forest. Her extensive studying of books on every plant she allowed in her forest soon made her an expert on anti-allergenic, silverfish-friendly vegetation.

Her silverfish village population reproduced rapidly. Soon Leonie had material to write her own encyclopaedia : LIVING LEGENDS FROM A SMALL, NON-GALLIC VILLAGE.. A side effect of her new lifestyle was that her allergies disappeared as if by magic.

Dr Grimmgold has dedicated his life to studying silverfish therapy.

13. **Martine Researches Men**

Last Wednesday, thanks to a favourable moon phase, relentless organising and sheer luck, Martine and Moony Mona met up for an evening of Mai Tais and observing men in their natural habitat.

The friends had begun RMR (Researching Male Repartee) back in college when they found listening in on the opposite sex more entertaining than any other hobby. Sure there were other collegiate sports: boxing, knitting, chess, drinking to excess, etc. but Martine and Mona had been set on their course of discovery since kindergarten.

Everything went smoothly at the Repartee Research Roundup on Wednesday. The singing of the RMR anthem[6*] was traditionally executed BEFORE the first cocktails, to avoid unpleasantness as decibel levels increased along with blood alcohol levels as the evening progressed. Martine and Mona stood to attention in their regulation oversized dark glasses and 4-inch spiky heels singing lustily:

> *"All is crazy, Everywhere madness!*
> *In vain I cast my glance on*
> *past and present,*
> *the reason ever seeking*
> *why men so fiercely fight*
> *with malice filled with spite!"*

[6*] further information on p. 47

Then came the second part of an RMR meet: detailed notes on the appearance of any men in range. Given the clothing and build of the only two available specimens, it wasn't hard to peg them as construction workers from the site across the way from this watering hole. Even without taking their work clothes into consideration, it was easy to guess that the tanned, muscular Schwarzenegger-types, already sporting substantial beer bellies, made their living knocking down and building stuff.

Slowly sipping their cocktails, Martine and Mona theorised in the MRM Field Notebook on probable discussion topics. Martine picked football and beer, while Mona, classifying them as fresh air fans, was convinced that hiking or scantily-clad DD beach bunnies was on the agenda.

After the first round of drinks it was time for the third RMR phase; getting up close.

The RMR rules mandated that they had to sneak up close enough to listen in on the specimens without making eye contact or getting invited over for a drink. If their cover was broken, they immediately had to move on to the next bar and start over - beginning with the anthem.

One lovely May evening back when the RMR founders were in their twenties, they had had to sing the RMR anthem SIX times before they successfully managed to eavesdrop. Now, with six decades on the odometer,

the experienced RMRers found it much easier to sneak up undetected to their chosen prey.
This Wednesday it only took Martine and Mona a few minutes to get within sneezing distance of the conversation. The ladies approached Phase 4: theoretical proof.

Our two hobby detectives listened to Karl-Heinz and Horst with bated breath. Everybody in the bar knew their names were Karl-Heinz and Horst because of their charmingly loud toast:
"KARL-HEINZ!!, (BURP!)",
"HORST!" (BU-U-URP!")
with every second gulp of beer.

Karl-Heinz was speaking in a deep, measured FM radio announcer voice, channelling former chancellor Helmut Kohl giving a eulogy:
"… but don't forget, you've got to sauté the onions first, before you even THINK of adding the diced zucchini and bell peppers. Have you ever tried marinating your chopped chanterelle mushrooms in champagne overnight?"

Finding their theories so wildly off the mark, the dedicated RMR ladies fortified themselves with the regulation Long Island iced teas and began to plan their next meeting.

* **Post Scriptum:** *the RMR anthem originates from the opera "The Meistersinger von Nürnberg", by Richard Wagner. This libretto could serve as the basis for a whole encyclopaedia of therapeutic applications or the development of a new wave of neuroses.*

14. Grouchy Nora

Sadly, Nora was not in a position to enjoy her life firsthand. NO: instead of dipping her tiniest toe in life's emotional whirlpool she wrapped herself up in an impermeable cocoon of fault-finding, with an extra layer of nit-picking. According to her very tolerant priest, she is the 2018-edition proof of the timeless truth of Matthew 7:3 -
> *"And why beholdest thou the mote that is in thy brother's eye, but considerest not the beam that is in thine own eye?"*

Because of her constant carping Nora has no friends: she's either stopped speaking to them or they fled from her interminable bitching - Nora's permanent default setting.

Today for the first time in her life Nora misses having someone to share her vicious griping as she starts clearing out her recently-deceased favourite aunt's apartment. Since Nora inherited her entire fortune, the rest of the family had no problem leaving her alone with the mess.

Where do you start cleaning out the home of someone you don't know well? Although Nora had liked her Aunt Elena, they weren't really close. The ladies enjoyed the occasional ritual tea together where they could JUST SIMPLY SIT THERE in the same room without having to maintain the required exhausting social pretence of expected emotions.

Nora was surprised to find a rather creative mess in her very orderly aunt's bedside table. Wanting to get the worst over with, she slipped on a pair of practical yellow rubber gloves (the family-size package had been on sale) and tackled the unpleasant task of sorting through it.

A major incongruity immediately caught her eye: a notebook bound in floral velvet. Aunt Elena had found time to write? There were two pink sticky-notes hanging out of it at a jaunty angle.
A closer look at the cover revealed gold embroidery: "FOR NORA IN CASE SHE HAS TO CLEAR OUT THIS LOT".

Surprised out of her normal truculence, Nora sat down on her aunt's uncomfortable bed to read :

"THERAPEUTIC PARTYING:
Some of the most wonderful moments of our lives are completely unexpected and unplanned. When you are feeling like a hamster on a wheel without any hope on the horizon of ever escaping the endless circle of boredom you just need to find some congenial guy, gal or companion to GET UP and PARTY DOWN with .

Stick the following note on your dressing table mirror to remind YOU to dress up every single day, put on your warpaint and BE READY TO GET UP and PARTY DOWN.

PARTY-DOWN, v.: to actively celebrate one's way out of a gross situation. It is possible to party one's way out of sadness, as long as one remains focussed on the

goal of well-being, religiously following the necessary steps of good planning, good friends, good food, and appropriate drink.
UNDER NO CIRCUMSTANCES waste PARTY DOWN time on oxygen thieves who just want to spread negativity and gloom!

VERY IMPORTANT when choosing your congenial companion:
Should you find one, marry him/her immediately or, at least strive for a life-time friendship.

*My grandmother always warned me against "**Negativos**"*
*She defined **Negativos** as people so invested in their gloomy outlook that they could find a catastrophic downside even in the headlines «WORLD PEACE AT LAST!» or « GLOBAL STARVATION: NOW ONLY PART OF HISTORY! »*

If world peace actually did break out, Negativos would probably be speculating about how the lack of war would inevitably cause economic collapse and unemployment. They would still have energy left to bemoan all the poor psychiatrists, lawyers, and fund-raisers recently put out of business by the annoying good fortune of their fellow man.

As my southern friends would say - "you could put that Negativo on Jesus' lap and he'd complain the Good Lord's knees were boney."

Please *stick the above definition on the inside of your front door as a warning notice. Keep Negativos out of your space! When you come home, read this note, and it will absorb and neutralise any lurking negativity trying to cross your threshold.*

Another antidote to contact with Negativos is to allow yourself FITS OF CONTENTMENT. Have you ever had one? Women's magazines write so much about super orgasms that I have the impression, plain old GENERAL SATISFACTION has been left wheezing in their dust.

My fits of contentment mostly surprised me when I was so low I didn't even have the energy to kill myself.

You go around complaining, determinedly discontent with life, your Weltschmerz radiating from deep in your left kneecap. Your leaden feet can hardly drag your listless carcass to and from work.
 Every exhausting breath appears to be a melancholy tax audit. Your budding depression is a nasty stepsister of the hellish, sticky, rude, uninvited guest who has no intent of ever leaving.

In THAT moment, dear Nora, when your body and soul have lost hope in life, then you are ripe for your own personal fit of contentment. Contentment wants to be invited in, Dearest!

Don't be a stranger to our birthright of contentment. Every day the media, restaurants, Big Business, and weather reports campaign hard for maintaining discontent. Advertisements blare that there is always something faster! more compact! more brightly coloured than whatever product we've just bought after years of careful savings.

The timing of a fit of contentment is a gift from God, dear Nora. Imagine you've just looked over your left shoulder to see what was bugging you and instead of ripping somebody's head, off you suddenly feel an overwhelming urge to roll around on a sweet meadow, purring like a playful kitten lazily hunting butterflies.

CONGRATULATIONS! This primal urge would be your a free fit of contentment. From the Great Beyond I sincerely wish you many more. If these lines have helped you, please spread the word!"

A smile slyly crept into Nora's eyes as she read Aunt Elena's quaint words. Soon she would be smiling so often that her face, used to years of sporting a grim, growling demeanour, would have occasional muscle cramps due to the unaccustomed smile perpetually invading Elena's wasteland of discontent.

On her way home to hang the heirloom notes as instructed, she popped into a stationary store to buy a little velvet notebook of her own.

Nora will leave posterity her own testimony of invoking content.

15. Olivia at the Opera

Olivia had only attended the opera because of her beloved Granny Anna's example and influence. But eleven years after Granny Anna had floated off to Valhalla, Olivia suddenly discovered that she actually *enjoyed* the performances.

She liked to invite younger friends to join her, not just for their shared pleasure but to pass along her grandmother's original South African Legend over cocktails - preferably Aperol Spritz.

When she gave books as presents, she usually wrote the Legend on the flyleaf for posterity.
Now that Olivia has joined her Granny in Valhalla, the legacy of Granny Anna may be, as stipulated in Olivia's will, shared with the general public.

Long live tradition!
*In South Africa there is a legend that tells of a bold band of heroic opera singers, who, faced with their adoring public's dearest desire: **change**, strove to fulfil it.*

Forth they went. Month after month these wild wanderers explored vast vistas of the Cultural Wasteland. They desperately sought a wondrous weapon against the overwhelming powers of darkest Dramaturgification*

In their quest for Enlightenment they found:
-Initiative,
-Pleasure in precision,

-Respect for all good craftsmen (musicians are CRAFTsmen too!), and
-Loyalty to one another to be the ultimate self-defence.

And so it came to pass that this merry mob of mutating Opera singers successfully threw themselves into a seemingly-impossible task - thereby utterly triumphing over maddening mediocrity.

And there was great rejoicing.

*Post Scriptum:
Granny Anna liked to use the word "DRAMATURGIFICATION" in all its declensions instead of resorting to foul language.
According to her personal pocket dictionary, **Dramaturgified:** *adj.* egregious, conceited, talentless, unwelcome.

16. Petra pulverises the Monday blues

Facing the 38th Monday of 2017 with a horrible head cold might have deflated all Petras creative survival instincts – if she hadn't had reliable, realistic friends who reminded her to accept every attack of germs or energy-vampire fellow human beings as an invitation to do a slow pirouette, blink twice and find the fourteen other options of looking at the latest challenge.

Scanning the full 360 degree spectrum of challenges life serves us, even without a preparatory pirouette, opens up countless possibilities of spring cleaning the physical and mental baggage we unknowingly treasure as necessary for our survival. If it is not to drag us down, the false security of habits and addictions we hide behind needs to be dusted and rearranged, or at least labelled for future action.

Enter prickly MONDAY:
Petra's defusing of the MONDAY CACTUS involves starting at the root of the problem. Tackling a seemingly insurmountable problem in small sections actually makes it manageable. Petra has discovered a simple, cost-effective antidote to neutralise threatening attacks of the Monday Blues in a ladylike fashion: **changing the perspective.**

Easy: Petra steps outside and consciously chooses the saddest view available. Last week, for example she focussed on the eternal construction site mess blighting the lush greenery in her neighbourhood, allowing herself be lowered into her already gaping bottomless pit of personal despair. Letting her tired eyes wander over the surrounding desolation, she discovered a tiny pink flower bravely grinning up at its own certain destruction. Then, changing her perspective from big-picture-blues to focus ONLY on the silly little pink flower, she grabbed her camera, zooming into the heart of a creature that would definitely be a casualty of the next onslaught of the construction workers.

Hash-tagging this picture with all the sadness that had been turning her Monday blue, she launched her change of perspective onto Instagram. The picture went viral and the sadness was absorbed by Instagram addicts.

After defusing the Monday Blues Petra switched off her phone; safe until at least the 39th Monday of 2017! When her horrible boss screamed in frustration at not being able to reach her during the exorcism, Petra sweetly blamed unspecified „updating problems", a story no amount of caterwauling could change.

Petra has become VERY creative about why she can NEVER be reached on Mondays.

17. Visiting quirky Queenie

Spending a night at Queenie's place is never dull. To start with, this confirmed bachelorette shares her apartment with three extremely spoiled felines who always stand front and center. Her decor really takes some getting used to - and that's putting it tactfully. Instead of paintings, curtains or tapestries, she hangs her walls with an eclectic, unashamedly eccentric collection of clothes and shoes and deconstructs her shelves with a fine, deliberate scattering of kitty-kitsch knick knacks.

Three days before your arrival you will receive her standard email to prep you for the experience.

"Looking forward to your visit in my cat-palace! Be prepared to join me in sloughing off everyday stress. Only pack clothing that will look even better when covered in cat fur. Please leave your troubles and your shoes outside on the pink WELCOME CATS carpet. Fluffy guest-slippers may be found to the right, behind the smaller cat tree, as you enter the foyer.

Our day revolves around the cats. In order to avoid misunderstanding, here is their daily routine:
1. *Before exiting the luxurious cat lounge, ALL limbs will be stretched in ALL directions* / FOR US: ditto + 50 pushups right where you rolled out of bed.
2. *Strut to the water bowl, disdain its condition* / US: thoroughly and reverently wash the bowl in question, fill the FINEST porcelain with the FINEST water and only

then seek the first coffee/tea/smoothie of the day. But before it can be drunk, an interruption is guaranteed...

3. *Slink around the food dish until a sumptuous meal appears* / US: Serve the cats breakfast then zip back to make the bed before they can capture it again, eat a handful of almonds while standing in front of the closet listening to the weather report and trying to decide what to wear - STARTING WITH THE SHOES OF COURSE!!!

4. *Complain about the condition of the litter box during prolonged and copious use before returning to the luxurious lounge* / US: Showering: 60 seconds, dressing: 24 seconds, makeup: one whole minute.

5. *Begin the first 3 hour grooming session in preparation for a hard day's napping* / US: THOROUGHLY brush the cats, lay out dry crunchies for snacking, work 12 hours to guarantee the cats may continue living in grandeur.

6. *Rise around 15:36, find a new opportunity for some therapeutic, willful destruction in the name of claw maintenance - extra points for creativity - then dedicate a lengthy purr to the goddess of the second round of napping: recommended duration of The Second Nap: 2 - 4 hours.* / US: A quick drink with buddies after work, then hurry home to perform the above prescribed steps 1-6 of the cat's Circle Of Life until death do you part."

Guests are encouraged to bring cat treats and kitty toys as hostess gifts.

18. Regina's Racehorse

Once upon a time a happy, very accomplished racehorse graced the stables of a big business. Although it wasn't an easy job, and left him little time to frolic around the pasture with his friends, Anouk loved everything about it: the tough daily training, no lolling about, getting up early in the morning for more workouts - the competition never sleeps...

Anouk was preparing for a very important race coming up at the Carousel Racetrack. Diet, rest, and the mental concentration that is so important to winning a race were honed to a razor's edge in readiness.

Two days ago Anouk's trainer surprisingly decided to try a new strategy:
one hour before the time trials hitched Anouk up to plow a field wearing a harness one size too small,
in the middle of the race he was made to stop an perform a dressage routine designed for a crippled donkey, and after the race he had to walk half the length of the track backwards - blindfolded.

In despair poor Anouk wonders what "strategic" obstruction, pretending to be professional preparation, will next be thrown at him.

Let us light a candle to his professionalism, good nature and sheer guts.

19. Sleepless on Sophia's Sofa

With the approaching full moon Sophia has had plenty of time to luxuriate in her insomnia. Anyone who says a full moon can't have an effect on people and their surroundings has obviously never had the fuzz blown out of their silly heads by the wild rush of a changing tide on a godforsaken beach.

During one of her bouts of insomnia Sophia was initiated into an environmentally friendly, endlessly renewable gift of energy by the call of a night bird. Anyone inquisitive and brave enough to follow her footsteps in this wild, liberating night can invoke this timeless, infinitely self-renewing power that is older than human memory.

Tracks in the sand tell the story:

First the tired, dragging prints, like the steps of the desolate condemned on the way to the scaffold. Then two deep impressions where Sophia stood motionless, rooted to the spot by the sight of powerful waves seeking to caress the swollen moon with long, foamy fingers.

Anyone not heedlessly speeding past this place of enlightenment would have sensed faint traces of the electric charge from the ocean's depths that infused every cell of Sophia's body. And then, the ecstatic fury of the simultaneous knowledge that one was always part of a benevolent universe, balanced by the ignorance of every cell in one's own mortal body that conjoins an infinite past and future horizon with the pragmatic NOW.

As a habitual full moon insomniac, Sophia has learned to channel this liberating, recyclable energy from her sofa. Of course she would prefer to be dancing naked on the beach during every full moon phase as she had done at her initiation but, sad to say, that won't pay the rent.

During full moon phases mostly Sophia sits on her shabby moon-colored couch and takes calls for her favourite suicide hotline.

The knowledge that flooded into her as she danced naked on that beach - knowledge which flourished and grew with every full moon - can thus be passed on anonymously to those whose consciousness has lost touch with its inherent self-healing power.

Although many of her suicidal callers were found dancing naked on some beach, they all eventually died of natural causes only - proudly wearing a contented moon smile on their lips.

20. Tina at the Tinguely-fountain = a farewell to self-imposed slavery

Life completed another circle for Tina at the Tinguely Fountain today.

Born a wandering nomad, Tina was always looking for compatible people to give her that rare feeling of kinship she so longed for. Basel should have been a place to drop some of her life's baggage, and take a breather. She had long since accepted that you cannot get rid of Life Luggage, but you can rearrange it, share it, decorate and hide it.

As a member of a traveling circus, Tina was used to regarding any spot on earth she found herself, be it Spitzbergen, Madagaskar, Venice, Cairo, Helsinki, or even Atlanta as <<HOME>>. With her infallible female logic and the basic attitude of a colonial conquerer, her philosophy could be summarised as: *"I'm standing on it, from now on it's mine"*. Living this motto implied that her feet were time-share owners of bits of real estate on all seven continents.

As Tina watched the 10 mechanical sculptures in "her" fountain, her mind'e eye reviewed her last 10 contracts with 10 different circus troupes.

The Tinguely Fountain had had a magical attraction for Tina ever since her circus student days in Basel. Whether she was in town to celebrate, mourn, or just relax, her wanderings inevitably led her to the Tinguely Fountain.

Whoever visits the fountain regularly, even without information gleaned from travel guides, Google & friends, will soon discover its melancholy side. The ten water-powered mechanical figures, built of scrap salvaged from the rubble of the theatre pulled down in August 1975, stand on the exact spot where actors, dancers and singers had once practiced their art.

Tina recalls the day she first became aware of the elegiac air around the Tinguely Fountain. She had just gotten back from a gig in Venice where, between rehearsals and performances, she had made a point of visiting Gunter Demig's "Stolperstein" plates commemorating Nazi terror victims. A respected colleague in Tel Aviv had recommended she explore the city this way, instead of just visiting the standard tourist traps.

Reading the inscribed stones in Venice had caused her to imagine the everyday life of the persecuted, and she could now sense a shadow of that in the comic fountain's machine people - a memorial to crushed hopes and repeatedly broken trust. The figurines unashamedly spouted their streams of mourning, sprinkling spectators with a priceless joie de vivre which persisted despite being surrounded by inappropriate humiliation, unprofessionalism, disappointment, and disrespect. Were these dancing fountains spouting the shadow of the tears of the artists who selflessly made their life's blood visible and audible to audiences until the old theatre was demolished in 1975?

Tina was leaving Basel the next day. She was especially drawn to one of the metal sculptures in the fountain - **"der Schaufler"**, the Shoveler. The little shoveler had always been her favourite character in the fountain pageant. The other figures are far too showy, wildly whirling and spraying jets of water around, but the focussed, hunched over little shoveler, tirelessly bails water with the ladles attached to his twig like arms. He concentrates on his task (emptying the fountain?) like a workaholic old ant trying to tidy up before retirement. For Tina he remains a visible synopsis of her professional wanderings. Today he cheekily reminds her: *"The circus is just your **job**, not real life!"*

Comforted, she can conclude this circle of communion with the fountain. A spiral rises out of the circle toward the heavens, offering infinite possibilities of new disappointments…and indestructible HOPE.

21. Uschi at the Dentist
Subtitle: The importance of good dental hygiene cannot be overstated

A beautiful young lady, dressed with an unfortunate dull sense of respectability, stared dreamily at the young dentist's latex-clad fingers as again and again, they brushed her soft, anaesthetised lips

Every movement of his crisply starched lab coat sent slow ripples of pleasure through her - from the crown of her lusciously long red hair right down to her left, finely manicured pinkie toe.

From the very first vibration of the drill, her fine, vulnerable scalp surrendered itself to sublime satisfaction.

Over and over again she looked up into the young dentist's luscious blue eyes. Framed by his functional face shield, they seemed to wink at her more intimately than the caress of a precious new lover at the first shared breakfast.

Uschi hates to miss a dental appointment.

22. Veronika:
enjoying life in bite-sized portions

If Veronica hadn't become a notorious TV chef she probably would have just spent her life making "bite-sized pieces" of every object and cultural event in her immediate vicinity.

Even as a child it was important to her to have all situations, literature, recipes, opera, and suchlike cut up into "bite-size pieces" so that she wouldn't miss out on even the tiniest pleasure when reading, cooking, listened or living. On the first day of school she learned she needed to hide her impatience - of maternal origin - and the curiosity obviously inherited from Dad. Her efficient solution: secretly using Lego blocks to build models of new experiences.

By puberty she did't need Lego any more; her flourishing imagination could effortlessly process and store intricate diagrams of everything new. Her parents, stolid, salt-of-the-earth people were overwhelmed by a daughter who wanted to put together cryptic snippets of all the great questions of Life at the breakfast table.

Luckily the family had a Good Fairy: Veronica's favorite aunt. She knew exactly when the strange little girl needed new stimulus. On Veronika's sixteenth birthday, Aunt Elinore thought it was time for the fledgling to take wing and presented her with a complete recording of Wagner's "DER RING DES NIBELUNGEN".

Veronika locked herself in her room with only rice cakes, water, and Wagner for sustenance and didn't come out until she'd listened to all sixteen hours of music. She couldn't quite envisage a diagram for what she'd just experienced, so she took the notebook that her o-so-omniscient Auntie had included with the recording, and wrote a condensed version of a gigantic work whose story usually takes 34 characters, a prologue, and three days to tell.

The Note-to-Self style subtitle of her condensed RING:
<u>Remove everything superfluous:
first build the foundation,
then hang the drapes.</u>

« A long time ago three Rhine Maidens (WOGLINDE, WELLGUNDE & FLOßHILDE) guarded magic gold in the Rhine. The Nibelung ALBERICH, a disgusting dwarf, stole the gold and, because he renounced love, could have his Nibelung brother MIME make a Ring out of it that would make him, the disgusting Nibelung ALBERICH, Master of the World.

When chief God WOTAN stole the Ring and leftover gold from ALBERICH, the Master of Meanness, to pay Messrs. FASOLT and FAFNER of Giant Construction Inc. for completing Valhalla, the gods' new multi-family house, ALBERICH, using powerfully obscene language, cast an eternal curse upon the Ring: "NOW LET ITS MAGIC BRING DEATH TO HIM WHO WEARS IT!!"

The moment the giants take possession of the ring its curse kicks in: FAFNER kills his brother FASOLT who is more interested in love than business, grabs the Ring and then happily turns himself in a monstrous wallowing worm.

Note: The curse can only be made null and void when the Rhine Maidens get the Ring back.

WOTAN's grandson, SIEGFRIED kills FAFNER, grabs the Ring and gives it to sweet, formerly divine BRÜNNHILDE, his aunt and bride, as a token of his undying love.
Under the influence of a magic potion SIEGFRIED takes the Ring back from BRÜNNHILDE and then gets murdered for his troubles by the Evil HAGEN, Alberich's ambitious bastard son.

So the widow BRÜNNHILDE gets to torch Valhalla and returns the stolen goods to the Rhine Maidens. »

Writing down this story set off a chain reaction in Veronika. She pondered how this tale could be served up as a dish that would make the new sensations experienced visible and, after consumption, part of one's very fibre. She could easily picture a diagram of the possible bodily changes enjoying a Ring-of-the-Nibelungs-delicacy might cause.

Since the forging of gold played such an important role in the story, she looked around for a recipe that would describe the blacksmith MIME's personality and workplace. She had to find a substance that would resemble molten gold in colour and texture and would call for extremely high temperatures in the preparation. Aunt Elinore cunningly suggested going for something sweet to balance MIME's grossly acidic nature and thought up the name MIME'S GOLD NUGGETS for the creation.

Veronika discovered a microwave recipe for the popular British candy, "Fudge" that was right on target. Making it required boiling sugar and butter together, reaching temperatures of over 200° C - admittedly far from the 1064° C required to melt gold, but still hot enough to command respect. Clearly a warning from the gods.

Inspired by the discovery of the recipe, Veronica was unstoppable. She energetically set to collecting recipes for all the gods, humans and animals that had amused her in the Nibelungen saga. As she happily gloated over her completed collection, she knew what to do with her life: redefine the concepts of cooking and eating for humanity.

The path to TV cook stardom was paved with stimulating obstacles. As she had already created a clear diagram in her head of how to reach her goal, success was assured.

She likes to encourage people to savour and relive her experiences with the RING DES NIBELUNGEN by sharing the following recipe that started her stellar, sensual rise to immortality:

MIME'S GOLD NUGGETS

Utensils:
1 microwavable bowl - HUGE, AS the mixture swells a lot when it boils.
1 wooden spoon to stir with
1 spoon-rest

Ingredients:
125 g butter or margarine
397 g sweetened condensed milk "Milchmädchen" or "Carnation" brand in Germany
573 ml sugar
5 ml vanilla extract

Instructions:
a) Combine butter, sugar and condensed milk in the bowl
b) Microwave for 2 minutes at FULL POWER
c) remove from Microwave, stir
d) Microwave for 5 minutes
e) repeat (c) and (d)
f) Remove from microwave, stir in vanilla extract
g) pour EXTREMELY HOT mixture into a lightly-buttered rectangular pan
h) Allow to cool, when it's tame enough to touch: hack into BITE-SIZED CHUNKS

It is recommended that the resulting crumbs be used to enhance musli, decorate ice cream or to attract well-meaning wandering gods & spirits.

23. Wilhelmine wanders the woods

In order to keep the little gears in her proud blonde head turning smoothly, Wilhelmina, along with some like-minded co-workers recently went for an extended hike in the forest. The group had a fine time traipsing up- and downhill, appropriately fortified with ample mead[7*].

The idea was to approach the gods of nature while feeling *quite* divine themselves. After a quick poll and a joyfully unanimous vote at a serious, short meeting, the club leadership had proclaimed mead to be the *only official* libation allowed on their outings.

About three hours into the hike, Wilhelmine spotted a 1962 Jaguar e-type parked near the trail. She left the group for a closer look. No problem with her crowd; the group had agreed to meet up again that evening at 6:30 sharp at THE WEIGHTY WANDERER pub for an asparagus and absinth dinner.

[7*]

Mead is an alcoholic beverage (much-loved by the Teutons) made of fermented honey, water and spices.
It will knock you on your derrière faster than you can say "Spätzlebrett".

As Wilhelmine leaned closer to admire the elegant interior of the dusty Jaguar, it gently whispered to her:

> "Just you wait and watch, my dear! The talent-free frauds of your nightmares will eventually be mown down by the wheels of time."

Relaxed and refreshed, she re-joined the company, and ordered a juicy cutlet to go with the delicious Baden-Wuerttemberg asparagus that has made THE WEIGHTY WANDERER world-famous.

Wilhelmine has become a feared food critic as well as an established vintage car photographer. Sad to say, she's still waiting for the nightmare to end.

24. XANTHIPPE

Whatever possessed Ms X's parents to name their cheerful, blonde, blue-eyed baby XANTHIPPE?
Xanthippe was a planned child. It took eight long years of fertility treatments before her parents conceived her under a full moon in Fuerte Ventura. At the time of the pregnancy, her 44-year old parents, Hans & Edna held full university professorships in chemistry. They were so proud of the functionality of their bodies and their reproductive success that by the fifth month of the pregnancy they had already bored their friends silly with details of the conception and the very exact plans for their yet-unborn child's life.

As Hans and Edna were both fluent in ancient Greek, they chose the child's name for its exact meaning: *Xanthippe* in the original Greek: Ξανθίππη, a combination of ξανθός xanthós „blond" and ἵππος híppos „horse"*. Hans and Edna's gene tests showed an 84% certainty their child would be a blond, muscular girl. So "Xanthippe", "blonde/yellow horse" seemed to them a fine name for their long-desired baby. Why it just ROLLED right off the tongue!

Had they been as familiar with history and literature as they were with the Periodic Table, they might have come across this passage in Nietzsche's tome ***Human, All Too Human:***

"433. XANTHIPPE
Socrates found the kind of woman he needed--but not even he would have sought her out had he known her well enough; not even the heroism of this free spirit would have gone that far. In fact, Xanthippe drove him more and more into his strange profession, by making his house and home inhospitable and unhomely…she taught him to live in the back streets, and anywhere where one could chatter and be idle, and in that way formed him into Athens' greatest backstreet dialectician, who finally had to compare himself to a pesky horsefly, set by a god on the neck of the beautiful horse Athens to keep it from coming to rest."

It wasn't until Xanthippe turned 31 - working as a streetcar driver, getting more hateful and surly by the day, that her parents realised how badly the name had affected their once sweet baby.

The very day after her birthday the Basel newspaper, THE DAILY NUTJOB, printed Dr. Berger's research on the "Xanthippe Syndrome", now called XANTIPATHY[8*]. Her parents were alarmed to recognise how well Xanthippe's character traits matched Dr Berger's list of the early warning signs of **XANTIPATHY:**

[8*] a total fabrication by Emiro von Berejesa †2019, who holds ALL intellectual property rights, including the publication rights of XANTIPATHY research. To view these wide-ranging reports, please submit a written request to Ansi Verwey-von Fleckenstein.

- In the early stages Xantipathy appears as simple mood swings.
- The more it progresses, the more easily a patient prevaricates.
- A fully developed Xantipant loses all ability to differentiate between truth and falsehood.
- Any attempt to demonstrate truth to the patient will result in outbreaks of unfounded and illogical rage.
- As the disease takes hold, the patient's voice becomes higher in pitch and the torrent of words increases. This is known as Xantipifivocalisation[9*].
- Xantipants noticeably lack grammatical awareness and display Dyslexic tendencies.
- One of the easiest ways to diagnose Xantipathy is by assessment of the patient's wardrobe.
A person exhibiting a marked inability to dress themselves appropriately could well be deluding themselves daily. If such a person had no friends to advise him/her on his/her clothes, this loneliness enables Xantipathy to progress to the point that the person develops into a full Xantipant.

Further research is needed to ascertain if Xantipathy is contagious in the workplace.

Hans and Edna needed to move quickly. Even without Dr Berger's formal diagnosis they were aware that

---

[9*] the ear-splitting orgiastic screaming indulged in by Xantipants.

Xanthippe hated people and that the feeling was mutual.

The famous University where they worked couldn't risk scandal. What would the DONORS think??

The threat of a possible contagion galvanised panicked politicians into mandating involuntary commitment into the Ministry of Health's new PROJECT XANTHIPPE institutions.

Just a week after Dr Berger's article on Xantipathy appeared, Xanthippe found herself in Siberia under the name "Ms X" - sentenced to life imprisonment in the high-security wing of an infamous mental asylum.

Thanks to a lavish donations, Dr Berger now has ample funding to pursue another 30 years of Xantipathy research.

25. Yolinda's Yodelling Horn

At first glance it would appear that our Yolinda cultivates a predictable, orthodox life. She merits closer scrutiny.

By day she goes to the conservatory on the hill where she dutifully instructs recalcitrant (and in some cases extremely untalented) students in the art of trombone playing. Don't be fooled by the fact that her work clothes are made exclusively of cotton. Nothing against cotton as a textile, but it is possible to give the skin a little change of pace with satin, velvet and such, as may easily be found at Yolinda's local branch of Silk, Satin & Co.

Warning for readers with an ironing allergy: Yolinda appeared at school EVERY DAY in collars and seams pressed and starched with a precision to make an army sergeant green with envy!

Sadly, first impressions stick, so her students nicknamed her THE IRONED TROMBONE and spread the rumour that she only took up the instrument as a subliminal substitute for those womanly curves of body and soul she lacked.

On weekends though, Yolinda shows her true colours - far from her usual conservative circles.

She did not want her students to encounter the flip-side of the Yolinda coin.

On weekends she was a talented and enterprising member of a band, **GOTH YÖDÆLLICĀ**, which toured the international graveyard circuit with their hardcore brand of extreme-sport-level Alphorn playing and yo-delling. The seven core members of this fearless group were all highly skilled in circus performance, yodelling, book-keeping, and playing the alphorn.

Book-keeping? Yes! Keeping international graveyard tour bookings running smoothly doesn't just mean detailed organisation, inspiration, hard practice sessions prepping new repertoire, and constant social media updates; it also means miles of paperwork and permits to ensure respectful and LEGAL events on those fascinating graves.

To stick to the milestones of future adventures only: Yolinda will unexpectedly run into Yuri, her school's soccer team captain, at a GOTH YÖDÆLLICĀ performance. Yuri's pet dachshund, Jürgli's funeral will trigger the encounter.

Tomorrow, after a hearty meal, a sated and content Jürgli will slumber on to his eternal reward. His master will have to scramble to make sure his Jürgli be laid to rest in a style befitting his admirable wiener dog life.

After great trouble and expense, **GOTH YÖDÆLLICÃ** will have acquired the necessary permits for a concert at exactly the time, in the exact same pet cemetery where darling Jürgli's mortal remains were to be interred with great ceremony.

It will take Yuri a long time to get over Yolinda's performance. His hormonally unstable constitution will need a while to process the vision and acoustic onslaught of "THE IRONED TROMBONE" in a shiny leather catsuit, her blonde hair flying, waving an ASSAULT ALPHORN, yodelling over the tiny pet tombstones.

Being a conscientious teacher , Yolinda will take Yuri aside and advise him that a cold shower and regular scale practice would be appropriate therapy to process the shock.

In six years, Yuri will be a world-renowned trombonist in the ranks of **GOTH YÖDÆLLICÃ**. His fashion choices will show a remarkable similarity to the THE IRONED TROMBONE'S graveyard stagewear.

26. Zippy Zoë:
Queen of Compromise Clothing

If COMPROMISE CLOTHING were an Olympic discipline, no airline in the world would accept Zoë's huge bag of gold medals as carry-on luggage - not even in First Class.

What a shame that you've never heard of COMPROMISE CLOTHING! Allow me to introduce you to it, using as an example model student Zoë, a lady with a highly developed sense of touch.

Compromise-clothing is far more than a simple choice of garment. Rather, it is a customised personal philosophy of Life that invites you to consistently question the EXPECTED, thereby contributing your bit towards saving everyday decency from extinction. Practicing conscious choice demands application and development of your own sensory perceptions.

For a simpler explanation, let's take a look at Zoë's glove collection. The substantial assortment of gloves embellishes one of her bedroom walls. Arranged systematically in orderly rows, clamped on their wire hangers with colourful clothes pegs, these accessories illustrate how the Fashion Industry frantically looks for something new, but always rediscovers the classics. The gloves nesting on lengths of retired bungee-cord that dangle like nervous jungle vines between the neatly sorted hand-wear seem poised for flight. They playfully offer Zoë a reminder to take off any residual mind-cuffs before choosing her gloves.

The sweet agony of choice shows her how a person can be seduced into hiding, enhancing, or even underlining their true Self; but also braced to rediscover self-confidence and strut out of their comfort zones.

On her bedside table an old etiquette guide book, draped in a shimmering green silk scarf from the 1930s, lies in state next to an assortment of self-devised miracle hand creams. When Zoë first noticed that she could detect, direct and consciously use energies through her hands, she began to care for them studiously. Her bedtime ritual for sweet dreams begins with a thorough hand cleaning, whereby she not only painstakingly removes any material dirt, but also repairs any spiritual maltreatment. Then, a mediative moisturising to celebrate that all the wear and tear of the day has been visibly dumped in the trash can. Under the canopy of her glove installation, she likes to read about 1930s hat and glove fashions as she falls asleep.

Thanks to her good hand care and mind-purifying bedtime reading, Zoë often dreams about which gloves will next protect, decorate or warn her. Her dreams are a magic potion that launches her out of bed, bouncy as a morning gazelle in spring, to choose her gloves for the envisioned compromises of the day - after just five hours of sleep and *before* coffee!

The conscious step to decide on her own terms what compromises she will make AND to display them -

disguised as gloves - to the world has spared her many hours of psychological therapy. Female logic: the money not needed to pay the shrink's bills is thereby available to be spent on more gloves.

Thus, she wears the crocheted brown gloves with mink cuffs to see her tax advisor, as a private memo to soldier elegantly through an unavoidable situation. The color brown reminds her to study bureaucratic regulations carefully until she can find some grey zones to entertain herself. The mink cuffs stand for a larger compromise in her life: to wear fur AT ALL. She had found these gloves at a flea market while spending a long weekend in Berlin with her friend Hannah.

Hannah convinced Zoë, an animal-loving lady, to buy the mink gloves DESPITE ALL with a simple calculation: a mink has a life expectancy of seven to ten years. So, if in 2010 you buy a mink pelt processed by some furrier in 1960, the creature has been running round on earth SIX times longer than Nature planned AND you are showing some respect for the endangered profession of furriers.

The compromise of owning a bit of fur led Zoë, who like many women freezes easily, to rummage around flea markets till she found the 1960s vintage mink coat she now LIVES in every winter. A side effect of wearing mink - the caress of it on her skin makes Zoë feel like a heroine in a Tolstoy novel set in Siberia.

Zoë is well aware of the effect wearing gloves has on those around her. When she and her neighbours slave away in their shared garden allotment, she gladly takes along a basketful of garden gloves in different patterns and sizes. This gift is not entirely unselfish: Zoë doesn't want to give up flaunting her own extravagant gardening gloves just to avoid disturbing the sensibilities of her more conservative fellow humans.

Her fun-loving grab bag of garden gloves has touched off a small epidemic of psychedelic garden wear among her neighbours. Those who enjoy a multicoloured Saturday clothing compromise as an alternative to their Monday to Friday gray-beige-brown camouflage quickly find the way to Zoë's weekly glove seminar in the British Teashop.

Should you ever run into Zoë, you'll undoubtedly recognise her self-confident bearing and inviting smile - matched with the inevitable uniquely entertaining, uncompromising gloves!

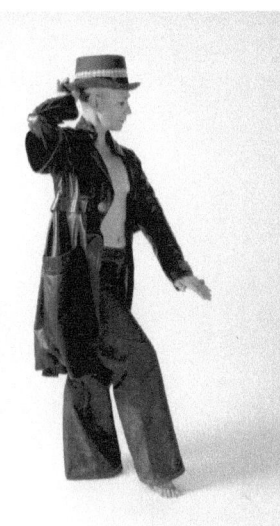

The author, Ansi Verwey - von Fleckenstein grew up on a farm in South Africa during the apartheid era.

Her urge to write was fostered by a juxtaposition of unstable political waves in an environment geared towards negating any shimmer of individuality.

On leaving Africa, the most important survival tool she took with her was an indestructible sense of humour.

Now a german citizen, this conductor, pianist and conférencieuse has practiced and defended her art across the globe, appreciating good music, good cuisine and exceptional people in i.a. Barcelona, Taipei, Hannover, Kapstadt, Lissabon, Stuttgart, Bilbao, Frankfurt, Pretoria, Basel, Atlanta und Wien.

A prime example of her approach to writing, life and music is never accepting that anything is impossible until she's tried it herself: in Dec. 2003 she was the Guinness world record holder in continuous piano playing; 52 hours and 59 minutes of playing music by Bach and Wagner have convinced her to question as unnecessary any restrictions the weather, society and her own expectations might impose on her.

Details about the current projects of this proud inhabitant of beautiful Hannover in Lower Saxony, Germany may be found on her website www.ansiverwey.de

www.ingramcontent.com/pod-product-compliance
Lightning Source LLC
Chambersburg PA
CBHW030449220526
45464CB00006B/2461